DUTCH OVEN

PIES

DUTCH OVEN PIES

SWEET & SAVORY

MATT PELTON

HOBBLE CREEK PRESS

An Imprint of Cedar Fort, Inc.
Springville, Utah

ISBN 13: 978-1-4621-1264-7

Published by Hobble Creek Press, an imprint of Cedar Fort, Inc.
2373 W. 700 S., Springville, UT 84663
Distributed by Cedar Fort, Inc., www.cedarfort.com

Library of Congress Cataloging-in-Publication Data on file

Cover design by Erica Dixon
Cover design © 2014 by Lyle Mortimer
Edited and typeset by Casey J. Winters and Rachel Munk

Printed in the United States of America

10 9 8 7 6 5 4 3 2 1

ALSO BY MATT PELTON

From Mountaintop to Tabletop

The Cast Iron Chef

The Cast Iron Gourmet

Up in Smoke

CONTENTS

INTRODUCTION

When I went to my first Dutch oven competition, I was amazed. My idea of a Dutch oven dessert was a boxed cake mix cobbler in a foil-lined Dutch oven or, if you were really fancy, a pineapple upside-down cake. Out of the twelve contestants, five of them were cooking pies in the Dutch oven!

"How are they going to pull this off?" I asked myself. I could not think of how someone could take a pie out of a Dutch oven, or even serve a slice of pie—this seemed to defy physics. As I took a step back and watched the competition, I was amazed by how these contestants did it: they left strips of parchment paper hanging from the lip of the Dutch oven; and, when the pie was done, they carefully lifted the pie out of the Dutch oven by those strips. The pies they produced did not look like traditional pies, but they were beautiful.

After that competition, I went home and immediately began cooking pies in my own Dutch oven. At first I didn't have much success; the pies did not remove easily from the Dutch oven. My crusts were often mealy and did not hold together. But when I face a challenge in life, I exploit it until it becomes a success. I had the same attitude with Dutch oven pies—I continued making them until it became second nature to me. I discovered that almost any ingredient can be made into a pie. The pastry crust is such a nice delivery envelope for so many sweet and savory dishes. I learned how to make amazing pastry dough, and discovered the ins and outs of perfecting the pastry.

1

In this book I have compiled all of my knowledge of pies and pastry and have broken it down for in an easy-to-learn manual. All of the recipes are tried and true, but feel free to experiment and put your own twist on them. I believe that, by experimenting, we can create many new and exciting dishes.

1
PIE CRUSTS

Pie crusts are a struggle for many people to perfect. However, they can be simple once you understand the basic principles of creating a pastry. All pastries follow a simple formula: two parts flour, one part fat, and just enough water to bind everything together. The flakiness of a crust depends on how the fat is mixed into the flour. If you blend it too much, you will get a mealy crust. If you don't mix it well enough, the crust will not hold together as it cooks and your pie will fall apart. The purpose of the water is to hold the pastry together, and should only be added a small amount at a time, just enough for the dough to be worked. The less water you use, the flakier your crust will be because you are allowing the fat to render, causing separation or flakiness. The fat used almost exclusively for pastry dough prior to the turn of the century was lard, which is still popular today, especially outside the United States. Today, a number of fats can be used other than lard, including shortening and butter. The fat you choose isn't significant, but it's helpful to know their unique qualities. For savory pies I prefer lard because of its unique flavor. When cooking a sweet pie I often use butter-flavored shortening because it is less expensive than butter and works a little better. Real butter is the king of fats for pastries because its flavor cannot be matched, but it can be costly. The milk fats in butter create richer pastries, but they also don't allow the pastry flake as well.

Learning to cut fat into flour is one of the most important components to making a fine pastry. For best results, cut the fat when it is cold rather than lukewarm. Using a pastry cutter is the best way to cut pastries. To use the cutter, mix the dry ingredients together in a shallow pitch bowl. Cut the fat into small pieces and distribute throughout the flour mix.

Fat ready to be cut into the flour.

Move the pastry cutter in rocking motions through the fat against the wall of the bowl. Turn the bowl each time you cut and continue until the fat is distributed into pea-sized or slightly larger chunks.

Many people swear by using a food processor to cut fat in. Just pulse the processor until the fat is pea-sized. I personally don't like this method even though it is faster. For me it is similar to using a mixer to knead bread or make pasta; it takes the personality out of the process. I gain so much from the feel of the dough that I can't get with a machine.

A lot of recipes call for salt. Salt is simply for flavor and doesn't do much more. Some pastry recipes call for a leavening like baking powder. Many claim that baking powder will cause separation and therefore flakiness. I do not find these ingredients necessary because a properly cut-in fat will do the same thing, but better, every time.

Fat dispersed in the flour. Note the pea-sized chunks of fat.

My favorite pastry recipe uses vinegar. I have seen a few that call for cream of tartar. These items are fabulous for creating a delicate, flaky pastry if you have proteins in the pastry. In my favorite recipe I also use an egg, which enriches the pastry with flavor, and allows the acid in the vinegar to isolate the egg protein and create separation in the pastry. The result is an ultra-delicate and flaky crust. Cream of tartar works the same way, especially when using butter instead of shortening. If you want to see an example of how this process works, whip some egg whites using a beater, with and without an acid. When you add cream of tartar, lemon juice, or vinegar, the egg whites will stiffen up much more quickly and will hold their shape. This trick will help you create a perfect meringue, as I will describe in a future chapter.

Some pastry recipes call for sugar. Like salt, it is only for flavor. Be frugal when using sugar; too much will prevent the pastry from separating correctly, especially if the sugar caramelizes from heat. The result will be a soggy, dense, and sweet crust that will not hold well and will appear greasy. I prefer the crust to be savory, allowing the fillings to add any desired sweetness. A savory shell will go a long way in balancing out the effect of a sweet pie filling.

After you have cut the fat into your pie crust, you need to fold in liquid to bind everything together. You can use water, milk, buttermilk, egg, vinegar, or any combination. Water is the simplest and most commonly used. Each liquid ingredient will give your pastry a different flavor and effect. Feel free to experiment until you find the mix that you prefer. Remember that you only need just enough moisture to bind the dough together and allow it to be worked. If your pastry is too wet, it will be difficult to work and your pastry will be dense. Use not enough liquid and it will be hard to work.

Liquid in the center of the dough, ready to be folded in.

Begin by creating a well in the center of your fat and flour. Add a little liquid and fold it into the dough. Knead the dough lightly. You should be able to form a ball that holds together, but breaks apart easily when you apply pressure to it. If it is too dry, you won't be able to form a ball. If you have too much liquid, the dough will be sticky and hard to handle. Most recipes you will find will be created for near sea-level. If you live at a higher elevation, you need to add a bit more liquid to start until you find the correct balance.

Once you have finished your pastry crust, you can chill it for up to three hours in the fridge if you are not ready to use it. When you begin, lay down a sheet of parchment paper and sprinkle it lightly with flour before rolling it out; if the pastry does not stick when you pull it up and lay it in a pie pan, your job will be much easier. Press the dough into the parchment paper and flatten it with the heel of your hand as best as you can. With a well-floured rolling pin, start rolling from the center of the dough out, turning the parchment paper a quarter of a turn each time as you do so. After the first four rolls, start to roll it out in one-eighth turns until the pastry is the desired thickness. I like to have it about an eighth of an inch thick. Work a baker's blade or a thin metal spatula underneath the pastry and fold the pastry to the middle. This will allow you to set it into a Dutch oven or make it into a pie form easily without tearing.

OLD-FASHIONED PIE CRUST

The most basic, original pie crust recipe still works well to this day. It makes enough pastry for one ten-inch pie with a full lid. This pastry works especially well for savory pies and tart apple pies.

2 cups white flour

1 tsp. salt

1 cup lard

¼ cup water

Mix the flour and salt together in a shallow bowl. Cut the lard in until it is in pea-sized chunks. Create a well in the flour and lard. Pour in the water and fold the flour into the water. Softly knead the dough together until you can form a ball. Let the dough relax for a few minutes to saturate before working into a pie shell. Press the dough firmly onto a well-greased board and roll it with a pin starting from the center, and roll out until the dough is about ⅛-inch thick and fairly round in shape. Place in a Dutch oven or pie pan, following the instructions in Chapter 2.

Finished open pie shell ready to be filled.

SOUTHERN-STYLE BUTTERMILK PASTRY

This rich pastry works well with a number of savory pies as well as sweet nut and custard pies like pecan pie. Its only disadvantage: it is not very healthy. This recipe will make three open-faced pies or two open-faced pie shells and one full lid.

3 cups flour

1 tsp. salt

½ tsp. cream of tartar

1–1½ cups real butter, chilled

1 egg

¼ cup buttermilk

Mix the flour, salt, and cream of tartar together in a shallow bowl. Cut the chilled butter in with a pastry cutter until the butter is in pea-sized chunks. Create a well in the flour and butter mix. Whip the egg and the buttermilk and pour into the well. Gently knead the dough together until you can form a ball. Let the dough relax for a few minutes to saturate before working it into a pie shell. Press the dough firmly into a well-greased board and roll it with a pin, starting from the center. Roll out until the dough is about ⅛-inch thick and fairly round in shape. Place in a Dutch oven or pie pan, following the instructions in Chapter 2.

MATT'S FAVORITE PIE CRUST

As the title suggests, this is by far my favorite go-to pastry for any type of pie. It has a delicate, flaky crust and tastes equally delicious with savory and sweet pies. The only downside to this crust is that it needs to be chilled.

3 cups sifted flour

1 tsp. salt

1–1½ cups butter-flavored shortening, chilled

1 egg, whipped

5 Tbsp. cold water

1 Tbsp. white vinegar

Sift the flour and salt together in a shallow bowl. Cut the chilled shortening into the flour with a pastry cutter until the pieces are slightly larger than peas. In a small bowl, whip the egg, water, and vinegar together. Create a well in the center of the flour-shortening mix. Pour the liquid in slowly and fold in the flour. Press and gently fold the mix together until it holds its shape. Let the pastry relax for at least 10 minutes before working it. Be sure to use plenty of flour on the surface as you work it or this mix will stick. To work it into a pie shell, press the dough firmly into a well-greased board and roll it with a pin, starting from the center. Roll out until the dough is about ⅛-inch thick and fairly round in shape. Place in a Dutch oven or pie pan, following the instructions in Chapter 2.

2
PASTRY TECHNIQUES

As discussed in the previous chapter, the way you mix the pastry is the key to success. Learning the proper techniques for working with pastry will make your life a lot easier.

When I first started making pies back in the mid-1990s, my fillings were amazing; but, as one friend told me, "You need a woman to make your crusts." My crusts were ugly and as dense as a brick. I finally learned how to mix the ingredients correctly, but then found out how hard pastry is to work with. It tore every time I picked it up, and it stuck to everything it touched. When I rolled out the pastry, the layers of fat separated and came off with the rolling pin, leaving a hole or a thin spot in the pastry. I found out that, like cast iron, the rolling pin needs to be seasoned and prepared properly. If you are using a wooden rolling pin, heat it up in a 200-degree oven for a few minutes and wipe it down with vegetable oil. When you are done using it, just wipe it off clean and put it away. If you need to wash it, use warm water and a small amount of soap, dry it immediately, and put a fresh coat of oil on the rolling pin (If you are using a silicone or a stone pin, they also need washing, but you won't need to season them like the wood). Once your pin is seasoned, the pastry won't stick like it did before.

The second technique will teach you how to roll out a crust. The first thing to do is lightly flour the surface that you are using to roll out the pastry. I have found that a large wood cutting board works the best for me. Place the pastry dough in the center of the board and

11

start to work it flat with your hands. Lightly sprinkle flour on top of the dough. Press the dough with your rolling pin, starting in the center and working it out. Turn the pin a quarter of a turn and roll it out again. Continue this as you roll until you have a large enough piece of pastry to work with. If the edges tear as you roll and it won't work for the size you are trying to roll out, use a little water on your finger and wipe the edges, fold them over, and roll them out again. There will be some separation in the pastry regardless of what you do. The trick is to roll out the pastry much larger than what you actually need.

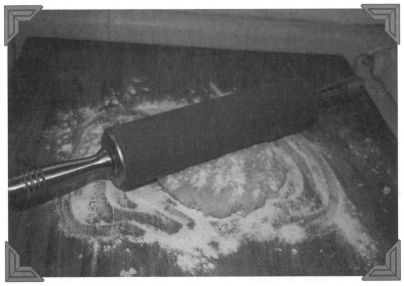

Flour the top of the pastry dough before rolling it out to prevent the pin from separating the dough.

Placing the crust into the pie tin or Dutch oven always frustrated me when I was younger. I was never taught how to do this, and at the time the Internet was not available to use as a reference. I would try to lift the crust off the board and place it in the pie tin. The problem with this is that it tore easily, and I often ended up patching the pie shell together afterwards.

The technique most often taught is to use the rolling pin to move the dough. Lay the rolling pin on top of the pastry dough. Start rolling the pastry onto the pin until you have the entire pastry dough rolled. Lay the rolling pin down on the Dutch oven or the pie tin and unroll the pastry onto the top. Carefully set the pastry dough into the pan and press it against the sides.

Start from one end of the skillet and unroll the pastry onto the pan.

But, before coming across this technique I came up with my own method. Despite learning the above technique for placing the crust into a pie tin, Dutch oven, or cast-iron pan, I still stick to using my tried and true method. To begin, I use a large metal spatula and work it underneath one half of the pastry dough. I then fold the edge of the pastry dough to the center of the dough. I work the spatula underneath the opposite half and fold it over as well. Then I do the same with the other two sides. I can then easily pick up the pastry dough and set it in the bottom of the Dutch oven or cast-iron pan. I then unfold the sides and press them to the edge of the pan (See page 14 for photos of this method).

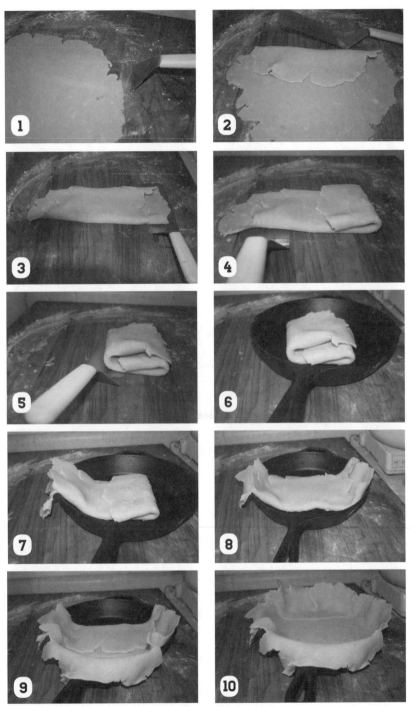

My method for placing crust into a pan.

There are a few different types of pie shells: open-faced, lattice-top, and full-top.

The open-faced shell is most common for custard-style pies. This is because the custard would not be able to cook properly with a closed pie crust.

The lattice-top pie is all about appearance, since the design does not help or hinder the taste or cooking procedure of the pie. Lattice-tops are most often associated with fruit pies because of how beautiful they look with the brightly colored fruit showing underneath.

Lattice-top fruit pie.

Full-top pies are the most functional because they trap in the flavors and hold the pie together. Venting a full pie shell is very important; otherwise, the pie will break, sometimes with great force, and can make a mess all over the oven.

When I used to make pies with a full crust, I used a fork to press the top and the bottom of the pie together. This didn't work as well as I would have liked, and often the seam between the top and the bottom would split and the filling would leak out. After that, I started using water to wipe the rim of the bottom pie shell before placing the top shell, making this procedure more successful for me.

I have had a lot of success antiquing the top, a process where you leave the bottom crust hanging over the edge, then folding it around the edge of the top crust. The problem with this method is that it isn't as pretty and can make the crust taste too heavy for the pie. It does work well for a number of savory pies, like pot pie, where a heavy crust can be a delicious addition. Now that I know how to properly crimp a shell, I can create a crust which works well with every kind of pie.

To crimp the shell, leave the top and the bottom long, and trim the edges to ½ inch farther than the edge of the pan. Fold the edges downward in half and use two fingers on your left hand to press a single finger on your right hand into the shell, forming a wavy crimp. This looks nice and is highly functional. You can buy tools to make different designs, but I like using my fingers.

Crimping the edge.

Many pie recipes in this book ask you to blind bake a pie shell. Blind baking is good for cold pies, in which you fill the shell with something that does not need to cook any longer. The problem I encountered with blind baking was that the crust would fall into the bottom of the pan, leaving me little or no crust on the sides and a very thick, flaky bottom. I tried many different methods and finally found my favorite. When you have your pie shell placed in the pan and the sides crimped, layer the inside of the pie shell with aluminum foil and fill with dried beans or rice. I use the same beans over and over again. This will hold the pastry in place and will allow you to blind-bake your shell. If you are cooking the crust completely, bake it at 375 degrees for 20–25 minutes. If you are blind baking a crust that will be baked again with a filling, like the crust for the crème brûlée pie (page 83), bake it at 375 degrees for 15 minutes. Let the pie crust cool down completely before pouring any filling into it.

To blind bake, line the pastry crust with foil and fill it with dried beans or rice. This will allow the crust to keep its shape as it bakes.

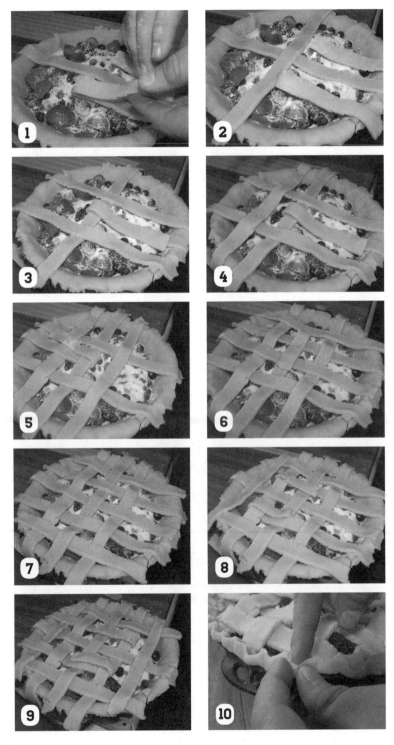

The process of latticework on a pie looks complicated, but it is actually very simple. You can start by just laying your strips one way and then the next, but if you learn the following trick of weaving lattice, you won't want to do it any other way. Start by laying three strips parallel across the pie—one in the middle and one on each side. Fold back the two lattice strips on the side, past the middle strip. Lay another strip of lattice perpendicular to the three, across the middle. Unfold the two lattice strips on the side and fold back the original middle strip. Lay the next two strips down on either side of the perpendicular strip. Follow this process until the pie is covered. If you want to create a diamond lattice instead of a traditional one, follow the same pattern, but lay the strips at an angle instead of perpendicular to each other.

3

HOW TO COOK PIES USING CAST IRON

I can't cook a pie anymore without using cast iron. There are so many advantages that I can't name them all. If I'm cooking at home, I like to use a ten-inch cast iron skillet; it is the right size and shape to make a perfect pie. If I'm in the mountains or cooking outside, the 10-inch does the job perfectly. There are advantages of cooking with cast iron: its natural non-stick quality, its superior heat control which keeps your pastry from burning before your filling is cooked, and its health benefits as your body absorbs the iron that cooks into your food.

If you're cooking a pie in the Dutch oven, one of the most difficult things to do is to remove it after cooking This is where parchment paper comes in handy. Cut two parchment paper strips, twelve inches long by four inches wide. Fold them in half and set them in the bottom of the Dutch oven. Cut a parchment round slightly smaller than the Dutch oven's diameter and set it down in the bottom on top of the two strips. Place your pastry crust in the pan as usual. When you close the lid to cook the pie, make sure the strips are between the lid and the pan. When the pie is done, carefully lift the two strips of parchment paper to remove the pie.

Cooking pies in a Dutch oven is amazing because of how easy it is to control the temperature. All of the recipes in this book were designed for a ten-inch Dutch oven or a ten-inch cast-iron skillet. With the Dutch oven, I have found that using eleven coals on the top in a checkered pattern and ten coals on the bottom in a ring sticking halfway out will maintain the 375 degree temperature that my recipes call for.

The temperature may vary depending on the conditions outside or your area's elevation, humidity, and so on. The great thing about a Dutch oven is that it doesn't matter; the pie will cook regardless. It will simply take longer to cook if it is cooler and quicker if it is hotter. The recipes in this book have descriptions of how to tell when the pies are done. Follow these and you shouldn't have any problems. If you end up cooking a pie for more than one hour, you'll need to refresh the coals to continue cooking.

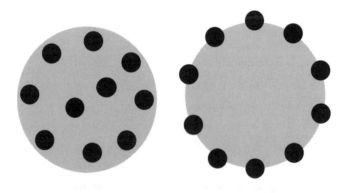

Top coal placement.   *Bottom coal placement.*

4

SAVORY PIES

• QUICHES •

Quiches are some of my favorite savory pies. A quiche is really just an omelet cooked in a pastry shell. Similar to an omelet, you can make just about any type of quiche easily. The base is simple: eggs, milk, flour, cheese, and whatever else you want to put in them. In this section I have included a few of my favorite quiche recipes. Enjoy!

TRADITIONAL COUNTRY QUICHE

This is a no-holds-barred country quiche. It is light and great for a morning brunch. This recipe makes one nine-inch quiche.

1 pie crust (see pages 3–10)

3 eggs, lightly beaten

1–1½ cups milk

¼ cup flour

¼ cup shredded Parmesan cheese

¼ cup shredded mozzarella cheese

1 tsp. black pepper

Prepare an open pie crust and lay it in the Dutch oven or pie tin. Mix all the remaining ingredients together and pour slowly into the pie crust until it is almost full. Bake at 375 degrees for 30–40 minutes, until the quiche is set and jiggles like well-set gelatin.

SPINACH QUICHE

There aren't many things I like better than fresh spinach with cheese and eggs. This is one of my favorite quiches. This recipe makes one nine-inch quiche.

1 pie crust (see pages 3–10)

3 eggs, lightly beaten

1 cup milk

3 Tbsp. flour

1 cup fresh spinach leaves, washed

½ cup shredded Cheddar cheese

¼ cup shredded Parmesan cheese

½ cup sour cream

1 tsp. onion powder

1 tsp. black pepper

Prepare an open pie crust and lay it in the Dutch oven or pie tin. Mix all the remaining ingredients together and pour slowly into the pie crust until it is almost full. Bake at 375 degrees for 30–40 minutes, until the quiche is set and jiggles like well-set gelatin.

HAM AND CHEESE QUICHE

This is my favorite quiche to make for breakfast. It is one of the most common quiche recipes, and for good reason. I love to eat it with fresh salsa on top.

1 pie crust (see pages 3–10)

4 eggs, slightly beaten

½ cup cream

1 cup milk

¼ cup flour

1 cup shredded Cheddar cheese

½ cup diced ham

1 tsp. black pepper

¼ cup shredded Parmesan cheese

Prepare an open pie crust and lay it in the Dutch oven or pie tin. Mix all the remaining ingredients together and pour slowly into the pie crust until it is almost full. Bake at 375 degrees for 30–40 minutes, until the quiche is set and jiggles like well-set gelatin.

MUSHROOM QUICHE

I love mushrooms! I'll eat any type and on almost anything. I could not compile recipes for quiche without including a mushroom quiche.

1 pie crust (see pages 3–10)

½ cup sliced and sautéed brown or portobello
  mushrooms

4 eggs

2 cups milk

3 Tbsp. flour

½ cup grated mozzarella cheese

¼ cup shredded Parmesan cheese

1 tsp. black pepper

4 oz. cream cheese, cut into small pieces

Prepare an open pie crust and lay it in the Dutch oven, pie tin, or cast-iron skillet. Sauté the mushrooms for 3 minutes in real butter. Mix all the ingredients except the cream cheese and mushrooms. Fill the pie crust with the egg and cheese mixture. Layer the cream cheese and mushrooms on top, spreading them evenly. Bake at 375 degrees for 30–40 minutes, or until the quiche is set like gelatin.

ITALIAN QUICHE

I tried this quiche when I was a kid and have loved it ever since. The sausage and tomatoes give it a whole new level of flavor. This recipe will make one nine-inch quiche.

1 pie crust (see pages 3–10)

4 eggs, slightly beaten

1 cup milk

3 Tbsp. flour

1/3 cup grated Parmesan cheese

1/2 cup grated mozzarella cheese

1/2 lb. sweet Italian sausage, cooked and chopped

2 oz. fresh basil leaves

2 roma tomatoes, finely diced

1 cup baby bella mushrooms, sliced

Prepare open pie crust and lay it in a Dutch oven or pie tin. Mix all the remaining ingredients together and pour mixture slowly into the pie crust until it is almost full. Bake at 375 degrees for 30–40 minutes, or until the quiche is set and jiggles like well-set gelatin.

BREAKFAST QUICHE

My dad made this quiche for us a few times when I was a kid. I love it because it contains everything in one breakfast dish. It is a little time intensive but it's worth it for a special treat.

1 pie crust (see pages 3–10)

4 eggs, slightly beaten

½ lb. diced potatoes, fried until well browned

½ lb. maple-flavored breakfast sausage links, cooked and sliced

1 cup milk

½ cup shredded Cheddar cheese

¼ cup flour

1 Tbsp. maple syrup

Prepare open pie crust and lay it in the Dutch oven or pie tin. Mix all the remaining ingredients together and pour the mixture slowly into the pie crust until it is almost full. Bake at 375 degrees for 30–40 minutes, or until the quiche is set and jiggles like well-set gelatin.

• POT PIES •

When most people think of a savory pie, pot pie comes to mind. I remember fondly the quick pot pies I made as a kid. They were frozen and from a box, but they provided a filling and tasty meal. Homemade pot pies are so much better—and better for you. Cast iron cannot be beat for cooking a pot pie. I often make them in a ten-inch skillet and throw them in the oven for an amazing dinner. One caution is to make sure the stew going into the pie is at room temperature. If it is hot, the fat in the pastry will separate early and will look messy.

CHICKEN POT PIE

Chicken pot pie is similar to beef pot pie, but is easier to bake from scratch since chicken is much more tender and cooks for less time.

  1 full-top pie shell (see chapters 1 and 2)

  3 Tbsp. flour

  3 Tbsp. real butter

  2½ cups water

  3–4 Tbsp. chicken base (available in most grocery stores in the soup aisle)

  1 small onion, cut into slivers

  1 lb. boneless chicken breasts or thighs, cut into bite-size chunks

  ½ cup carrots peeled and cut into small thin rounds

  ½ cup celery cut into small pieces

  2 bay leaves (remove bay leaves after turning the heat off and allowing stew to cool)

  1 tsp. black pepper

  salt to taste

Begin by creating a roux in the bottom of a Dutch oven or a saucepan: whisk the flour into the butter for several minutes over medium-high heat until the roux is dark blond in color and you can smell the flour cooking. This step is important for thickening and flavor. Immediately add the water and whisk it until it is thick. Mix the chicken base into the roux mixture.

In a separate skillet, sauté the onion until it is clear. Add the chicken and brown on high heat until it is solid white. Add the chicken and onions to the roux. Add the remaining ingredients, cover, and stir every once in a while until the chicken has become tender—this should take about 30 minutes. (Add a slurry of corn-starch and water if the stew is too thin. This needs to be added when the stew is at a boil—stir it in slowly until it reaches the desired consistency.)

Turn off the heat and let the stew cool to slightly warmer than room temperature. Lay the pie shell in a skillet or Dutch oven, keeping the sides high. Slowly ladle in the stew into the pie shell. Carefully lay a lid of pastry on top of the stew. Fold and crimp the ends of the shell and lid.

Cut 2–3 vent lines in the pastry lid (I like to cut them along the lines I will cut to serve). Brush the top of the shell with an egg wash (1 egg and a splash of milk mixed well).

Bake at 375 degrees for 30–40 minutes or until the crust is golden brown. Let the pie rest for several minutes before serving.

BEEF POT PIE

I usually make beef pot pie the day after I make a beef stew. Using leftovers makes this recipe quick and easy. The pot pie also gives variety to the leftovers. I will give you the recipe as if from scratch, but if you have a leftover stew or want to use a can of stew, simply bake it in a pie shell and you are done.

1 full-top pie shell (see chapters 1 and 2)

3 Tbsp. real butter

3 Tbsp. flour

2½ cups water

3 Tbsp. beef base (available in the soup aisle of most grocery stores)

1 small onion, cut into small slivers

1 lb. beef stew meat, cut into bite-sized chunks (I prefer using beef chuck)

½ cup thinly sliced celery

½ cup carrots, sliced into thin rounds

2 cups new potatoes cut into bite-size chunks (use a high-sugar potato like red, Yukon gold, or fingerling to prevent the stew from becoming too starchy)

2 bay leaves (remove the bay leaves after you turn the heat off and allow the stew to cool down)

1 tsp. black pepper

salt to taste

Begin by creating a roux in the bottom of a Dutch oven or a saucepan: whisk the flour into the butter for several minutes over medium-high heat until the roux is dark blond in color and you can smell the flour cooking. This step is important for thickening and flavor. Immediately add the water and whisk it until it is thick. Stir the beef base into the roux mixture.

In a separate skillet, sauté the onion until it is clear. Add the beef chunks to the onions and brown it on high heat until it is very well browned. Add the beef and onions to the roux. Add the remaining ingredients, cover, and stir every once in a while until the beef has become tender. This may take 1 hour to accomplish. (Add a slurry of cornstarch and water if the stew is too thin. This needs to be added when the stew is at a boil—stir it in slowly until it reaches the desired consistency.) Turn off the heat and let the stew cool down to slightly warmer than air temperature.

Prepare a pie shell and lay in a skillet or Dutch oven, keeping the sides high. Slowly ladle the stew into the pie shell. Carefully place the pastry lid on top of the stew. Fold and crimp the ends of the shell and lid. Cut 2–3 vent lines in the pastry lid (I like to cut them along the lines I will cut to serve). Brush the top of the shell with an egg wash (1 egg and a splash of milk mixed well). Bake at 375 degrees for 30–40 minutes or until the crust is golden brown. Let the pie rest for several minutes before serving.

STEAK AND MUSHROOM POT PIE

This is my go-to beef pot pie because it is so quick and easy to make. Using a decent cut of meat is important, because the cook time is too short to tenderize the meat. I like to use a sirloin cut, which is fairly inexpensive but is great for medium length cook times like this.

1 full-top pie shell (see chapters 1 and 2)

3 Tbsp. flour

3 Tbsp. real butter

2½ cups water

3 Tbsp. beef base

½–1 small onion, sliced into slivers

3 garlic cloves, diced

1 lb. beef sirloin, cut into strips

1 lb. baby bella mushrooms, cut into chunks

¼ tsp. cumin

1 tsp. black pepper

Begin by creating a roux in the bottom of a Dutch oven or saucepan: whisk the flour into the butter for several minutes over medium-high heat until the roux is dark blond in color and you can smell the flour cooking. This step is important for thickening and flavor. Immediately add the water and whisk it until it is thick. Stir the beef base into the roux mixture.

In a separate skillet, sauté the onion and garlic until the onion is clear. Add the beef strips and mushrooms to the onions and garlic, and brown it on high heat for 2 minutes. Remove from the heat. Add the beef, garlic, mushrooms, and onions to the roux. Add the cumin and pepper. Turn off the heat and let the stew cool to slightly warmer than room temperature.

Prepare a pie shell and lay in a skillet or Dutch oven, keeping the sides high. Slowly ladle in the stew into the pie shell. Carefully place the pastry lid on top of the stew. Fold and crimp the ends of the shell and lid. Slice 2–3 vent lines in the pastry lid (I like to cut them along the lines I will cut to serve). Brush the top of the shell with an egg wash (1 egg and a splash of milk mixed well).

Bake at 375 degrees for 30–40 minutes, or until the crust is golden brown. Let the pie rest for several minutes before serving.

CREAMY CHICKEN POT PIE

This recipe is similar to the chicken pot pie but with a cream sauce and a wild rice blend. It takes a little longer to cook but is well worth the time. I often make this the day after I make chicken wild rice soup, using the leftovers so it is quick and easy to make.

1 full-top pie shell (see chapters 1 and 2)

3 Tbsp. flour

3 Tbsp. real butter

2 cups milk

2 Tbsp. chicken base (available in grocery stores in the soup aisle)

1 lb. boneless skinless chicken thighs with fat removed, cut into chunks

½ sweet onion, cut into slivers

2 oz. wild rice blend, prepared according to package directions

¾ cup celery and carrots sliced thin, with celery leaf included

2 oz. Cheddar cheese, shredded

½ cup cream

Create a roux in the bottom of a Dutch oven or a saucepan: whisk the flour into the butter for several minutes on medium-high heat until the roux is dark blond in color and you can smell the flour cooking. This step is important for thickening and flavor. Immediately add the milk and whisk it until thick. This mixture is a béchamel. Mix the chicken base into the béchamel.

In a separate skillet, sauté the onion until it is clear. Add the chicken chunks to the onions and brown it on high heat until the chicken is a solid color. Add the chicken and onions to the béchamel. Add the remaining ingredients except the cheese and cream. Cover and stir every once in a while until the chicken has become tender. This should take about 30 minutes. Turn off the heat and let the stew cool down a little. Add the cream and slowly stir in the cheese.

Lay the pie shell in a skillet or Dutch oven, keeping the sides high. Slowly ladle the stew into the pie shell. Carefully lay the pastry lid on top of the stew. Fold and crimp the ends of the shell and lid. Slice 2–3 vent lines in the pastry lid. (I like to cut them along the lines I will cut to serve). Brush the top of the shell with an egg wash (1 egg and a splash of milk mixed well).

Bake at 375 degrees for 30–40 minutes, until the crust is golden brown. Let the pie rest for several minutes before serving.

CHICKEN AND DUMPLINGS PIE

This recipe is similar to the chicken pot pie with the exception that the top pastry shell is replaced by a layer of buttermilk dumplings.

1 pie shell (see pages 3–10)

3 Tbsp. flour

3 Tbsp. real butter

2½ cups water

3–4 Tbsp. chicken base (available in most grocery stores in the soup aisle)

1 small onion, cut into slivers

1 lb. boneless chicken breasts or thighs, cut into bite-size chunks

½ cup carrots peeled and cut into small, thin rounds

½ cup celery cut into small pieces

2 bay leaves (remove before baking)

1 tsp. black pepper

salt to taste

For the dumplings:

2 cups flour

1 tsp. salt

1¼ tsp. baking powder

¼ tsp. cream of tartar

½ cup real butter

½ cup buttermilk

Begin by creating a roux in the bottom of a Dutch oven or saucepan: whisk the flour into the butter for several minutes over medium-high heat until the roux is dark blond in color and you can smell the flour cooking. This step is important for thickening and flavor. Immediately add the water and whisk it until it is thick. Mix the chicken base into the roux mixture.

In a separate skillet, sauté the onion until it is clear. Add the chicken chunks to the onions and brown on high heat until they are solid white. Add the chicken and onions to the roux. Add the remaining ingredients, cover, and stir every once in a while until the chicken has become tender. This should take about 30 minutes. (Add a slurry of cornstarch and water if the stew is too thin. This needs to be added when the stew is at a boil—stir it in slowly until the desired consistency is achieved). Turn off the heat and let the stew cool down to slightly warmer than air temperature. Remove the bay leaves from the stew.

Prepare the dumplings by mixing all the dry ingredients together in a shallow bowl. Cut the butter into the flour using a pastry cutter until the butter is in pea-size chunks and dispersed throughout the flour. Create a well in the middle of the flour and butter mixture. Add the buttermilk to the well and fold the flour and butter into the buttermilk. Fold the dough gently just until it is all bound together.

Lay the pie shell in a skillet or Dutch oven, keeping the sides high. Slowly ladle the stew into the pie shell. Roll out and drop the buttermilk dumplings on top of the stew.

Bake at 375 for 30–40 minutes, or until the crust is golden brown. Let the pie rest for several minutes before serving.

LEFTOVER TURKEY POT PIE

This amazing after-holiday meal can be made fairly quickly with a little planning. It is also a great way to use up leftover turkey.

1 full-top pie shell (see chapters 1 and 2)

1 small onion, sliced into small slivers

2 cups new potatoes cut into bite-size chunks (use a high-sugar potato like red, Yukon gold, or fingerling to prevent the stew from becoming too starchy)

1 lb. leftover turkey, cut into small chunks

2 cups leftover turkey gravy

2 tsp. cornstarch

½ cup frozen corn kernels

Prepare the pie crust and lay it in a Dutch oven or a cast-iron skillet with plenty of extra crust over the sides. In a skillet, sauté the onions until they are clear.

Add the potatoes and cook for 15 minutes, until the potatoes are browning slightly and becoming tender. Put the potatoes and onions into the pie shell and add the remaining ingredients.

Cover the pie with a pastry lid. Crimp the edges of the shell and lid and cut slits for venting the pie (I like to cut them along the lines I will cut to serve). Brush the top of the pie with an egg wash (1 egg and a splash of milk mixed well).

Bake the pie at 375 degrees for 30–40 minutes, or until the crust is golden brown. Let the pie rest for several minutes before serving.

• VEGETABLE PIES •

CAULIFLOWER CHEESE PIE

I am a fan of cauliflower in a cheese sauce. This pie is one of my favorite side dishes.

> 1 full-top pie shell (see chapters 1 and 2)
>
> 3 Tbsp. flour
>
> 3 Tbsp. real butter
>
> 2 cups milk
>
> 1 lb. cauliflower, washed and cut into bite-size pieces
>
> ½ tsp. pepper
>
> ½ cup cream
>
> ¼ cup shredded Parmesan cheese
>
> 1 cup shredded Cheddar cheese

Create the roux by whisking the flour into the butter for several minutes over medium-high heat until the roux is dark blond in color and you can smell the flour cooking. This step is important for thickening and flavor. Immediately add the milk and whisk it until it is thick; this mixture is called a béchamel. Stir the cauliflower into the béchamel. Add the pepper. Cover and stir every once in a while, cooking for about 30 minutes.

Turn off the heat and let the stew cool down a little. Add the cream and slowly stir in the cheese. Lay the pie shell in a skillet or Dutch oven, keeping the sides high. Slowly ladle the mixture into the pie shell. Carefully lay the pastry lid on top. Fold and crimp the ends of the shell and lid. Slice 2–3 vent lines in the pastry lid (I like to cut them along the lines I will cut to serve). Brush the top of the shell with an egg wash (1 egg and a splash of milk mixed well).

Bake at 375 degrees for 30–40 minutes, until the crust is golden brown. Let the pie rest for several minutes before serving.

MUSHROOM PIE

As mentioned before, I love mushrooms of all types. This pie is full of mushrooms. It also contains a ragù that I used to win my second Dutch oven world championship title.

1 shallot, sliced thin

1 full-top pie shell (see chapters 1 and 2)

3 lbs. mushrooms (I use a variety: baby bellas, chanterelles, shiitakes, trumpets)

½ cup cranberry juice

1 (6-oz.) pkg. demi-glace (available online or at high- end grocery stores)

¼ cup fresh grated Parmesan cheese

Sauté the shallot in a little oil until it just starts to brown. Add the mushrooms and sauté until they are sweating. Deglaze the pan with the cranberry juice. Slowly stir in the demi-glace and simmer for 20 minutes, until the liquid is beginning to become thick. Turn off the heat and let it relax for several minutes.

Lay a pie crust in your Dutch oven or cast-iron skillet. Scoop the ragù into the prepared pie shell and layer the top with the Parmesan cheese. Roll out a pastry lid and Carefully place it on the top. Fold and crimp the ends of the shell and lid. Cut 2–3 vent lines in the pastry lid (I like to cut them along the lines I will cut to serve). Brush the top of the shell with an egg wash (1 egg and a splash of milk mixed well).

Bake at 375 degrees for 30–40 minutes, until the crust is golden brown. Let the pie rest for several minutes before serving.

CREAMY SPINACH PIE

I love spinach! Creamy spinach is by far my favorite way to eat it. This pie tastes great paired with roasted chicken.

    1 full-top pie shell (see chapters 1 and 2)
    3 Tbsp. flour
    3 Tbsp. real butter
    2 cups milk
    1 lb. spinach, washed
    2 cloves garlic, chopped
    ½ tsp. pepper
    1 lemon peel, zested
    ½ lemon, squeezed
    ½ cup cream
    ¼ cup shredded Parmesan cheese

Create a roux in the bottom of a Dutch oven or a saucepan: whisk the flour into the butter for several minutes over medium-high heat until the roux is dark blond in color and you can smell the flour cooking. This step is important for thickening and flavor. Immediately add the milk and whisk it until it is thick; this mixture is called a béchamel. Stir the spinach and garlic into the béchamel. Add the pepper, lemon zest, and lemon juice. Cover and stir every once in a while. Cook for about 30 minutes.

Turn off the heat and let the stew cool a little. Add the cream and slowly stir in the cheese. Lay the pie shell in a skillet or Dutch oven, keeping the sides high. Slowly ladle the mixture into the pie shell. Carefully place the pastry lid on top of the stew. Fold and crimp the ends of the shell and lid. Slice 2–3 vent lines in the pastry lid (I like to cut them along the lines I will cut to serve). Brush the top of the shell with an egg wash (1 egg and a splash of milk mixed well). Bake at 375 for 30–40 minutes, or until the crust is golden brown. Let the pie rest for several minutes before serving.

NEW POTATO AND PEA PIE

When I was growing up, my dad used to make pea and new potato soup with fresh homemade rolls. I could smell it cooking from outside when I came from school. It remains one of my favorite comfort foods. I converted that recipe into a pie and it turned out great. Enjoy!

1 full-top pie shell (see chapters 1 and 2)

3 Tbsp. flour

3 Tbsp. real butter

2 cups milk

2 (14-oz.) cans whole new potatoes, or 1 lb. small red
    potatoes; washed and cubed

8 oz. frozen or fresh peas

2 tsp. sugar

1 tsp. black pepper

salt to taste

½ cup cream

Create the roux by whisking the flour into the butter for several minutes over medium-high heat until the roux is dark blond in color and you can smell the flour cooking. This step is important for thickening and flavor. Immediately add the milk and whisk it until it is thick; this mixture is called a béchamel. Stir the potatoes and peas into the béchamel.

Add all remaining ingredients except the cream. Cover and stir every once in a while, cooking for about 30 minutes, or until the potatoes are fork tender (this will take less time if you use canned potatoes). Turn off the heat and let the mix cool a little. Add the cream and slowly stir.

Lay a pie shell in a skillet or Dutch oven, keeping the sides high.

Slowly ladle the mixture into the pie shell. Carefully place the pastry lid on top of the mix. Fold and crimp the ends of the shell and lid. Slice 2–3 vent lines in the pastry lid (I like to cut them along the lines I will cut to serve). Brush the top of the shell with an egg wash (1 egg and a splash of milk mixed well).

Bake at 375 degrees for 30–40 minutes, until the crust is golden brown. Let the pie rest for several minutes before serving.

CHILE RELLENO PIE

Chile relleno is my favorite Mexican food. Every time I go to a Mexican restaurant I want to try something else on the menu, but always end up eating the relleno. Figuring out how to make it into a pie was difficult, but it turned out delicious.

1 pie shell (see pages 3–10)
5–7 chile passillas (or anaheims); seeded, deveined,
    and cut into slices
1 lb. queso fresco
8 oz. shredded Mexican cheese blend
1 (8-oz.) can medium enchilada sauce

Begin by roasting the chiles in the Dutch oven until they are starting to wrinkle. Prepare a pie shell and place in the bottom of the Dutch oven or cast-iron skillet. Trim and crimp the edge of the pie crust. Layer the bottom with chiles, followed by the queso fresco and a little of the Mexican cheese blend. Follow this process until the pie is nearly full. Carefully pour the enchilada sauce over the chiles and cover with the remaining Mexican cheese blend.

Bake in a 375-degree oven for 30–40 minutes, or until the cheese and crust are browned. Let it rest for 15 minutes to allow it to set before serving.

RATATOUILLE PIE

Long before the movie of the same name, I enjoyed ratatouille. It reminds me of summer with all those fresh garden vegetables.

1 pie shell (see pages 3–10)

1 yellow squash, sliced thin

1 zucchini, sliced thin

1 small eggplant, sliced thin with the skin left on

3 vine-ripened tomatoes

1 red bell pepper, veins and seeds removed, cut into strips

3 cloves garlics, minced

2 Tbsp. chopped parsley

1 tsp. thyme

salt and pepper to taste

8 oz. mozzarella cheese

After prepping all of the veggies, prepare a pie crust and place it in the Dutch oven or cast-iron skillet. Layer the veggies one type at a time in the pie crust, and sprinkle with the garlic, parsley, thyme, salt, and pepper. Sprinkle the cheese on top. Crimp the edge of the pie crust and bake at 375 degrees for 30 minutes. The veggies should be tender and the crust browned.

• MEAT PIES •

FRENCH MEAT PIE

This is a great pie to make if you have leftover mashed potatoes. It is a classic pie that makes a great and unique main course.

1 pie shell (see pages 3–10)
1 small onion, sliced thin
½ lb. ground beef
½ lb. ground pork
2 cups mashed potatoes
½ cup mushrooms, chopped fine
1½ tsp. allspice
2 tsp. salt
1 tsp. black pepper

Put the onion in a skillet and brown well. When they are browned, mash them well. Add the beef and pork to the onions and cook until browned. In a mixing bowl, mix the meat and remaining ingredients together.

Place the pie crust in a Dutch oven or cast-iron skillet. Fill the pie shell with the meat mixture. Carefully lay the pie lid across the top of the pie. Slice 2–3 vent lines in the pastry lid (I like to cut them along the lines I will cut to serve). Brush the top of the shell with an egg wash (1 egg and a splash of milk mixed well).

Bake at 375 degrees for 30–40 minutes, until the crust is golden brown. Let the pie rest for several minutes before serving.

MEAT LOAF PIE

I am not a huge fan of meat loaf because I have eaten a lot of bad meat loaf in my time. I was about to swear it off forever, but I decided there was no reason I shouldn't like them because I love meatballs, and essentially meat loaf is just a large meatball. I decided what I didn't like about it was the garish overcooked ketchup so many people put on the top. Because of this, I will not include ketchup in this recipe. If you want to put it on, go ahead. I am sure that once you try a meat loaf pie, you will enjoy it as a new twist on a classic.

1 full-top pie shell (see chapters 1 and 2)

½ sweet onion, sliced

1 lb. lean ground beef

½ lb. ground pork

½ cup bread crumbs

½ cup mushrooms, chopped fine

2 eggs

Put the onions in a skillet and brown well. When they are browned, mash them well. Add the beef and pork to the onions and cook until browned. In a mixing bowl, mix the meat and all the remaining ingredients together.

Place the pie crust in a Dutch oven or cast-iron skillet. Fill the pie shell with the meat mixture. Carefully lay the pie lid across the top of the pie. Slice 2–3 vent lines in the pie lid (I like to cut them along the lines I will cut to serve). Brush the top of the shell with an egg wash (1 egg and a splash of milk mixed well).

Bake at 375 degrees for 30–40 minutes, until the crust is golden brown. Let the pie rest for several minutes before serving.

ITALIAN MEATBALL PIE

This is a fun and unusual pie. I have never seen a meatball pie before, so I thought it would be exciting to create.

    1 full-top pie shell (see chapters 1 and 2)
    1 lb. ground beef
    ½ lb. ground pork
    2 tsp. chopped parsley
    5 cloves garlic, minced
    1 tsp. oregano
    ½ cup Italian-style bread crumbs
    ¼ cup fresh grated Parmesan cheese
    2 eggs
    1 (24-oz.) bottle marinara sauce of choice
    8 oz. shredded mozzarella cheese

Begin by mixing all the ingredients together except the marinara sauce and the mozzarella cheese. Form the mixture into meatballs. In a skillet, heat up a little oil and brown the meatballs well. Lay the pie shell in a Dutch oven or cast-iron skillet. Arrange the meatballs on the bottom, cover with the marinara sauce, and sprinkle the mozzarella cheese over the top. Carefully lay the pie lid on top of the pie. Slice 2–3 vent lines in the pastry lid (I like to cut them along the lines I will cut to serve). Brush the top of the shell with an egg wash (1 egg and a splash of milk mixed well). Bake at 375 degrees for 30–40 minutes, until the crust is golden brown. Let the pie rest for several minutes before serving.

SWEDISH MEATBALL PIE

This is the Italian Meatball Pie (page 49) but with a white sauce.

1 full-top pie shell (see chapters 1 and 2)
For the meatballs:
1 lb. ground beef
½ lb. ground pork
2 tsp. chopped parsley
1 tsp. onion powder
½ tsp. garlic powder
¼ cup mushrooms, chopped
½ cup bread crumbs
2 eggs

For the sauce:
3 Tbsp. flour
3 Tbsp. real butter
2 cups milk
1 tsp. salt
1 tsp. black pepper

Begin by mixing all the ingredients together and forming them into meatballs. In a skillet, heat up a little oil and brown the meatballs well. In a separate Dutch oven, create a roux by whisking the flour into the butter for several minutes over medium-high heat until the roux is dark blond in color and you can smell the flour cooking. This step is important for thickening and flavor. Immediately add the milk and whisk it until it is thick; this mixture is called a béchamel. Add the salt, pepper, and the browned meatballs. Cook on low heat for 15 minutes. Let the mixture cool.

Lay the pie shell in a Dutch oven or cast-iron skillet. Arrange the meatballs on the bottom and cover with the white sauce Carefully roll out a pastry lid and set on top of the pie. Slice 2–3 vent lines in the pastry lid (I like to cut them along the lines I will cut to serve).3 Tbsp. flour

Brush the top of the shell with an egg wash (1 egg and a splash of milk mixed well).

Bake at 375 degrees for 30–40 minutes, until the crust is golden brown. Let the pie rest for several minutes before serving.

MEDITERRANEAN CHICKEN PIE

This pie reminds me of a stuffed pita bursting with flavor.

1 full-top pie shell (see chapters 1 and 2)

1 lb. boneless skinless chicken breasts, cut into strips

salt and pepper to taste

4 cloves garlic, minced

2 oz. fresh basil leaves

8 oz. fresh spinach leaves, washed

2 oz. feta cheese, crumbled

2 tsp. balsamic vinegar

1 vine-ripened tomato, sliced thin

2 oz. mozzarella cheese, shredded

1 cup plain yogurt or sour cream

Sauté the chicken in a little olive oil until the chicken is solid in color. Add the salt and pepper and balsamic vinegar. Place the pastry shell into a Dutch oven or a cast-iron skillet. Layer all the ingredients into the shell one at a time, making sure there is yogurt between the layers. Carefully lay the pie lid on top of the pie. Slice 2–3 vent lines in the pastry lid. (I like to cut them along the lines I will cut to serve.) Brush the top of the shell with an egg wash (1 egg and a splash of milk mixed well). Bake at 375 degrees for 30–40 minutes, until the crust is golden brown. Let the pie relax for several minutes before serving.

• SAVORY CUSTARD PIES •

A custard pie is similar to a quiche but lighter in texture. The trick to cooking a custard pie is knowing when to pull it out of the oven. Chefs teach a lot of different techniques, but I have found the best way is to jiggle the pie. If it sloshes like a water balloon, it is not done. If it has a firm jiggle like a well-set gelatin, it is done. If it doesn't move, it is overcooked.

CORN CUSTARD PIE

I love the flavor of a freshly made southern-style cream corn. That is the inspiration for this pie. Fresh-picked corn works best; however, frozen sweet corn works as well, and the result will still be amazing.

1 pie shell (see pages 3–10)

4 eggs, mixed well

1 cup cream

1 cup milk

1 tsp. salt

2 tsp. sugar

1 lb. fresh corn or frozen sweet corn

In a large bowl, mix all the ingredients together except the corn. Mix well for several minutes. Slowly fold the corn into the custard.

Place the pastry shell in a Dutch oven or a cast-iron skillet. Crimp the edges of the crust and slowly pour the custard into the shell.

Bake at 375 degrees for 40–50 minutes, until the custard is set and the crust is brown.

SWEET ONION CUSTARD PIE

For this pie, using the right kind of onions is important. You want to use sweet onions such as New Mexico sweet, walla walla, or sweet Mayan. Look for onions that are wider than they are tall—this will be a mature onion that has converted most of its starches into sugars. The result will be a sweet pie with an onion ring-type flavor.

1 pie shell (see pages 3–10)

4 eggs, mixed well

½ cup cream

1½ cups of milk

1 tsp. salt

1 tsp. sugar

1 large sweet onion, cut into thin slivers and caramelized

In a large bowl, mix all the ingredients together except the onions. Mix well for several minutes. Sauté the onions in real butter on medium heat until the onions are clear and starting to brown. Slowly fold in the onions into the custard.

Place the pastry shell in a Dutch oven or a cast-iron skillet. Crimp the edges of the crust and slowly pour the custard into the shell.

Bake at 375 degrees for 40–50 minutes, until the custard is set and the crust is brown.

SPINACH AND MUSHROOM CUSTARD PIE

I love spinach and mushrooms. When you put them together in a savory custard pie? Mmmm-good!

1 pie shell (see pages 3–10)

4 eggs, mixed well

1 cup cream

1½ cups milk

1 tsp. salt

1 tsp. black pepper

1 tsp. hot sauce (I like Frank's original)

8 oz. brown mushrooms, cut into strips

8 oz. fresh spinach leaves, washed and drained

In a large bowl, mix all the ingredients together except the spinach and mushrooms. Mix well for several minutes. Sauté the mushrooms in real butter on medium heat until they start to brown. Slowly fold in the spinach into the mushrooms. Cook them for 2 minutes, then stir them into the custard. Place the pastry shell in a Dutch oven or a cast-iron skillet. Crimp the edges of the crust and slowly pour the custard into the shell. Bake at 375 degrees for 40–50 minutes, until the custard is set and the crust is brown.

CHEESY BROCCOLI CUSTARD PIE

Cheddar broccoli is one of my favorite soups. I converted this dish into a mouthwatering custard pie.

1 pie shell (see pages 3–10)

4 eggs, mixed well

1 cup milk

1½ cups cream

2 tsp. salt

1 tsp. black pepper

1 lb. fresh broccoli cut into florets

4 oz. Cheddar cheese, shredded

In a large bowl, mix all the ingredients together except the broccoli and cheese. Mix well for several minutes. Sauté the broccoli in real butter on medium heat until they sweat. Cook them for 2 minutes more, then stir them into the custard. Slowly fold the cheese into the broccoli and custard. Place the pastry shell in a Dutch oven or a cast-iron skillet. Crimp the edges of the crust and slowly pour the custard into the shell. Bake at 375 degrees for 40–50 minutes, until the custard is set and the crust is brown.

• JUST-FOR-FUN PIES •

I had to do a section of just-for-fun pies that I really couldn't fit anywhere else in the book. I have only listed a few, but you can make almost anything into a pie.

CHILI AND CORNBREAD PIE

The only thing better than chili and cornbread is a chili and cornbread pie. You can make this quickly using canned chili and a cornbread mix if time is an issue. I've included some of my recipes from scratch.

1 pie shell (see pages 3–10)

For the chili:
1 medium onion, peeled and kept whole (remove before putting in the pie)
1 lb. beef stew meat, cut into bite-size pieces
¼ lb. breakfast sausage links, cut into bite-size chunks
1 (14-oz.) can pinto beans, rinsed and drained
1 (14-oz.) can black beans rinsed and drained
2 bay leaves (remove before putting in the pie)
1 tsp. garlic powder
1 tsp. cumin
1 tsp. black pepper
1 tsp. ground red pepper (optional)
2 cups water
2 tsp. beef base
2 Tbsp. cider vinegar

For the cornbread:

1½ cups yellow cornmeal

2½ cups milk

1½ cups white flour

1½ tsp. baking powder

1½ tsp. baking soda

¼ tsp. cream of tartar

2 tsp. salt

½ cup white sugar

½ cup brown sugar

3 large eggs

8 Tbsp. real butter, melted

Begin at least 2 hours ahead. Add all the ingredients for the chili into a Dutch oven. Let it simmer for 2–3 hours, stirring every few minutes, making sure that nothing sticks to the bottom of the pan. Add water as needed to make sure it won't burn. If the chili is not as thick as you would like, mash the beans with a potato masher to thicken. Remove the chili from the heat. Mix all the ingredients together for the cornbread. Set aside. Lay the pie shell into a Dutch oven or a cast-iron skillet. Crimp the edges and fill the shell halfway full of chili. Slowly pour the cornbread mix on top. Bake in a 375-degree oven for 40–50 minutes, until you can stick a knife into the cornbread and it comes out clean.

TACO PIE

This is one of those strange pie ideas my kids suggested. The pastry makes a great substitute for the tortilla. I have added some tortilla chips for flavor. I like to garnish this pie with sour cream, fresh tomatoes, and avocados. This recipe calls for chicken, but you can easily substitute ground beef if you would like.

1 pie shell (see pages 3–10)

1½ lbs. boneless skinless chicken breasts, cut into small chunks

½ lime, squeezed

1 (1-oz.) packet taco seasoning (available in the spice or Hispanic food aisles of many grocery stores)

½ cup medium salsa

corn tortilla chips (enough to cover the pie)

4 oz. shredded Mexican cheese blend.

Sauté the chicken in a skillet until it is almost solid white in color (there should be plenty of moisture left in the pan). Add the lime juice and the taco seasoning packet. Cook for an additional 2 minutes on medium heat. Remove the chicken from heat and stir in the salsa.

Place the pie shell in a Dutch oven or cast-iron skillet. Crimp the edges and fill the pie shell with the chicken and salsa mixture. Layer the tortilla chips on top of the chicken and cover them with cheese.

Bake at 400 degrees for 30 minutes, until the crust is browned and the cheese is bubbly and browning.

LASAGNA PIE

This recipe tastes like a mix between a calzone and lasagna.

1 pie shell (see pages 3–10)

8 oz. dry lasagna noodles

1 lb. Italian sausage; cooked, drained, and cut into small pieces

4 cloves garlic, minced

8 oz. baby bella mushrooms, sliced

1 (20-oz.) jar marinara sauce

8 oz. ricotta cheese

1 egg

1 tsp. salt

1 tsp. pepper

1 tsp. oregano

8 oz. mozzarella cheese, shredded

Boil the lasagna noodles until they are still a little firm to the bite (al dente). In a skillet, sauté the sausage, garlic, and mushrooms until the sausage is well browned. Pour in the marinara sauce and remove the skillet from the heat. In a separate bowl, mix the ricotta cheese, egg, salt, pepper, and oregano. Lay the pie shell in a Dutch oven or a cast-iron skillet. In the bottom of the pie shell, spoon a layer of the ricotta cheese mix, followed by the sausage and marinara, a portion of the mozzarella cheese, and a layer of noodles. Repeat this pattern at least once more until the pie shell is filled. Finish the process with the remaining mozzarella cheese on top.

Bake the pie at 400 degrees for 30–40 minutes, until the crust is golden and the cheese is bubbly and browned. Let the pie rest for 20 minutes before serving.

TAMALE PIE

I love tamales, but they are so labor intensive to make that I reserve them for special occasions. For this pie, however, the process doesn't take long at all and it tastes amazing.

1 pie shell (see pages 3–10)

For the chicken mix:
1 lb. boneless skinless chicken breasts, cut into strips
1 lime, squeezed
1 tsp. cumin
2 tsp. New Mexico chili powder
2 cloves garlic, minced
1 tsp. salt
1 (8-oz.) can Rotel original tomatoes
1 (2-oz.) can diced green chiles

For the topping:
2 cups masa (a fine ground cornmeal found in the
    Hispanic aisle of the grocery store)
1 tsp. salt
¾ cup butter-flavored shortening
1 cup warm chicken stock
1 (8-oz.) pkg. corn husks, soaked in water

Sauté the chicken in a skillet until it is almost white. Add the remaining chicken mix ingredients and cook for 5 minutes on medium heat. Remove from the heat and let it cool. In a bowl, mix the salt into the masa. Cut in the shortening until it is dispersed well. Add the chicken stock and whip it up. The masa mix should be spongy.

Lay the pie shell in a Dutch oven or cast-iron skillet. Layer the bottom of the pie with the chicken mixture. Spoon the masa mix over the top and cover with a layer of the wet corn husks.

Bake for 30 minutes at 375 degrees. Let the pie set for several minutes before serving.

CHICKEN CORDON BLEU PIE

Chicken cordon bleu is so good, and in a pie it's amazing. I added a little spinach to this recipe because it is a good contrast to the cheese and chicken.

1 full-top pie shell (see chapters 1 and 2)

2 Tbsp. flour

2 Tbsp. butter

1 cup milk

1 tsp. salt

1 tsp. black pepper

1 lb. boneless skinless chicken breasts, cut into strips

½ lemon, zested and squeezed

4 oz. fresh spinach, washed and drained

4 oz. mozzarella cheese, shredded

8 oz. ham, cut into small pieces

½ cup sour cream

Create the roux by whisking the flour into the butter for several minutes over medium-high heat until the roux is dark blond in color and you can smell the flour cooking. This step is important for thickening and flavor. Immediately add the milk and whisk it until it is thick; this mixture is called a béchamel. Add the salt and pepper to the béchamel and turn it down to low heat.

In a skillet, sauté the chicken until it is almost white. Add the lemon zest and squeeze the lemon juice into the chicken. Add the spinach and stir it until it is beginning to go dark. Slowly stir the cheese into the béchamel sauce until it is melted and smooth. Fold the chicken and spinach mixture into the béchamel. Add the ham and sour cream. Remove it from the heat and allow it to cool. Lay the pie shell in a skillet or Dutch oven, keeping the sides high. Slowly ladle the mixture into the pie shell. Carefully place the pastry lid on top of the mix. Fold and crimp the ends of the shell and lid. Slice 2–3 vent lines in the pastry lid (I like to cut them along the lines I will cut to serve). Brush the top of the shell with an egg wash (1 egg and a splash of milk mixed well). Bake at 375 degrees for 30–40 minutes, until the crust is golden brown. Let the pie rest for several minutes before serving.

5

SWEET PIES

Sweet pies are what most people think of when they imagine pie. I have assembled several sweet pies from my favorites and a few others that were experiments gone well. Some recipes are similar because they have a common base, so I have also included a low-sugar pie recipe. You can convert any of these recipes to low-sugar versions by substituting a low-calorie sweetener in place of the sugar, divided by one-third because the artificial sweeteners pack a lot more punch. I like to substitute most of the sugar with sweetener but keep some of the sugar for flavor and texture.

• FRUIT PIES •

A fruit pie is simple to make. All it takes is some fresh fruit, sweetener, and something to thicken it. Most fruit contains enough liquid to create a nice sauce for the pie. When using fruit that is naturally very sweet I recommend using cider vinegar, sherry vinegar, or lemon as well; otherwise the pie can become too sweet and will be taste more like candy than pie.

STRAWBERRY RHUBARB PIE

Of all pies, this is my favorite. The rhubarb and strawberries create a perfect balance of flavor.

    1 pie crust (see pages 3–10)
    3 cups thinly cut strawberries
    2 cups thinly cut rhubarb
    1½ cups sugar (substitute ¾ cup sugar with Stevia for
        a low-sugar pie)
    ¼ cup instant tapioca pudding mix
    ¼ cup flour

Mix all the ingredients together. Let it sit for 15–20 minutes. The liquid from the fruit should partially dissolve the sugar. Pour the fruit into the pie crust in the Dutch oven. Level and settle the fruit as well as possible. If you are making a full-shell pie, carefully roll out a pastry lid and set on top of the pie. Slice 2–3 vent lines in the pastry lid (I do these along the same path I would cut it to serve). If you choose a lattice top, cut the lattice into strips and lay them out in one of the patterns found on page 19. Brush the top of the shell with an egg wash (1 egg and a splash of milk mixed well). Bake at 375 degrees for 30–40 minutes, until the crust is golden brown. Let the pie rest for several minutes before serving.

LOW-SUGAR STRAWBERRY PIE

In Alaska in the summertime I crawled around on my hands and knees in the meadows eating as many wild strawberries as I can grab. I plan to take some home for baking, but they are so good I can't help but eat them. Needless to say, I have never made a wild strawberry pie. Instead I take store-bought strawberries and turn them into something amazing when I bake them into a pie. This is a low-sugar pie, but you can use 1½ cups sugar instead of the sugar and sweetener.

> 1 pie crust (see pages 3–10)
> 6 cups strawberries sliced thin lengthwise
> ½ cup sugar
> ⅓ cup Stevia sweetener
> 3 Tbsp. cornstarch
> 1 Tbsp. sherry vinegar

Place the prepared pie crust in a Dutch oven or cast-iron skillet. Mix the ingredients together and pour them in the pie shell immediately. Flatten them out as best as you can.

If you are making a full-shell pie, carefully roll out a pastry lid and set on top of the pie. Slice 2–3 vent lines in the pastry lid (I do these along the same path I would cut it to serve).

If you choose a lattice top, cut the lattice into strips and lay them out in one of the patterns found on page 19.

Brush the top of the shell with an egg wash (1 egg and a splash of milk mixed well).

Bake at 375 degrees for 30–40 minutes, until the crust is golden brown. Let the pie rest for several minutes before serving.

CHERRY PIE

The cherry pie has been around for years, and for good reason. The difficulty arises when you don't have fresh cherries and you have to choose between canned cherries or unripe table cherries. If you try to use ripened table cherries, they will become too soft in the mix and become indistinguishable. This recipe uses not-quite-ripe table cherries. They will taste great and are much more accessible than pie cherries.

1 pie crust (see pages 3–10)

1 lb. not-quite-ripe cherries, cut in half, pits removed

2 cups sugar

juice of 1 lemon

1/3 cup flour

Place the prepared pie crust in a Dutch oven or cast-iron skillet. Leave the edges long. Mix the ingredients together and pour them in the pie shell immediately. Flatten them out as best as you can.

If you are making a full-shell pie, Carefully lay the pie lid on top of the pie. Slice 2–3 vent lines in the pastry lid (I do these along the same path I would cut it to serve).

If you choose a lattice top, cut the lattice into strips and lay them out in one of the patterns found on page 19.

Brush the top of the shell with an egg wash (1 egg and a splash of milk mixed well).

Bake at 375 degrees for 30–40 minutes, until the crust is golden brown. Let the pie rest for several minutes before serving.

BLUEBERRY PIE

Southeast Alaska is known for its blueberries. Every time my family visits, we go picking and bring home as many as we can. Most of them end up in muffins and pancakes, but occasionally I will make a blueberry pie.

1 pie crust (see pages 3–10)

1 lb. fresh blueberries

1½ cups sugar

¼ cup tapioca instant pudding mix

3 Tbsp. cornstarch

Place the prepared pie crust in a Dutch oven or a cast-iron skillet. Leave the edges long. Mix the ingredients together and put them in the pie shell immediately. Flatten them out as best as you can.

If you are making a full-shell pie, carefully roll out a pastry lid and set on top of the pie. Slice 2–3 vent lines in the pastry lid (I do these along the same path I would cut it to serve).

If you choose a lattice top, cut the lattice into strips and lay them out in one of the patterns found on page 19.

Brush the top of the shell with an egg wash (1 egg and a splash of milk mixed well).

Bake at 375 degrees for 30–40 minutes, until the crust is golden brown. Let the pie relax for several minutes before serving.

MIXED BERRY PIE

This is one of my go-to fruit pies because you can buy packages of frozen mixed berries at almost any grocery store. This makes creating a delicious pie quick and easy.

1 pie crust (see pages 3–10)

5 cups frozen mixed berries

1½ cups sugar

3½ Tbsp. cornstarch

Place the prepared pie crust in a Dutch oven or a cast-iron skillet. Leave the edges long. Mix the ingredients together and put them in the pie shell immediately. Flatten them out as best as you can.

If you are making a full-shell pie, carefully roll out a pastry lid and set on top of the pie. Slice 2–3 vent lines in the pastry lid (I do these along the same path I would cut it to serve).

If you choose a lattice top, cut the lattice into strips and lay them out in one of the patterns found on page 19.

Brush the top of the shell with an egg wash (1 egg and a splash of milk mixed well).

Bake at 375 degrees for 30–40 minutes, until the crust is golden brown. Let the pie rest for several minutes before serving.

PEACH PIE

When I think of late summer nights I think of a fresh peach pie cooling in the window, its aroma wafting in the summer air. My mouth starts to water in anticipation of the sweet juicy peaches and the perfect flaky crust.

1 pie crust (see pages 3–10)

5 cups peaches with the skins removed and cut into slices (to remove the skins, blanch the peaches in boiling water for 2 minutes)

1½ cups sugar

¼ cup flour

1 tsp. cinnamon

Place the prepared pie crust in a Dutch oven or a cast-iron skillet. Leave the edges long. Mix the ingredients together and put them in the pie shell immediately. Flatten them out as best as you can.

If you are making a full shell pie, carefully roll out a pastry lid and set on top of the pie. Slice 2–3 vent lines in the pastry lid (I do these along the same path I would cut it to serve).

If you choose a lattice top, cut the lattice into strips and lay them out in one of the patterns found on page 19.

Brush the top of the shell with an egg wash (1 egg and a splash of milk mixed well).

Bake at 375 degrees for 30–40 minutes, until the crust is golden brown. Let the pie rest for several minutes before serving.

• APPLE PIES •

We've all heard the idioms: as simple as apple pie, or as American as apple pie. These are both amusing to me because these apple pies are not simple, they're definitely not indigenous Americana. What *is* true is that apple pies are a crowd pleaser, and apple pie recipes are as countless as the stars, most being passed down from one generation to another.

CARAMEL APPLE PIE

A caramel apple pie is a beautiful thing. This pie tastes like a candy caramel apple in a pie shell.

1 pie crust (see pages 3–10)

2 apples, sliced thin, skin removed

2 Tbsp. butter

2 tsp. cinnamon

2 Tbsp. sugar

4 eggs, slightly beaten

1 cup dark corn syrup

²/₃ cup sugar

½ cup butter, melted

1 tsp. vanilla

Saute the sliced apples for 10 minutes in 2 tablespoons of butter on medium heat. Add the cinnamon and sugar and stir well. Remove the mixture from the heat. Separately, mix all remaining ingredients together in a bowl. Lay the prepared pie crust in a Dutch oven or cast-iron skillet. Carefully pour the caramel mixture into the pie shell. Lay the apples in the caramel mixture. Crimp the edge of the pie shell and bake at 375 degrees for 40 minutes. The caramel should be well set when you jiggle it. Let the pie cool and set for at least 20 minutes before serving.

DUTCH APPLE PIE

The main difference between this pie and the All-American Apple Pie (page 74) is the topping. For this pie, instead of a full crust you create a type of pastry crumble.

1 pie crust (see pages 3–10)

For the apples:
4 cups thinly sliced, deseeded, and skinned tart
   apples, such as Granny Smiths
1 cup brown sugar
½ cup sugar
1 tsp. cinnamon
3 Tbsp. flour
1 tsp. salt

For the topping:
½ cup flour
½ cup sugar
8 Tbsp. real butter

Lay the prepared pie crust in a Dutch oven or a cast-iron skillet. Crimp the edges and set aside. In a separate bowl, mix the flour and the sugar for the topping and then cut the butter in with a pastry cutter. Mix together the ingredients for the apples and lay them in the bottom of the pie shell. Layer the crumble mix on top of the apples.

Bake at 375 degrees for 35–40 minutes. The crust should be a deep golden brown. Let the pie rest for several minutes before serving.

ALL-AMERICAN APPLE PIE

You can't compile a book about pies and not include a classic American apple pie. Most recipes use only green apples, but I like to use a mix.

1 pie crust (see pages 3–10)

2 lbs. Granny Smith apples

½ lb. red apples, like Fuji

3 Tbsp. flour

2 tsp. cinnamon

½ tsp. nutmeg

½ cup brown sugar

1 cup white sugar

Lay the prepared pie crust in a Dutch oven or a cast-iron skillet. Leave the edges long. Slice the apples thin and combine with the remaining ingredients. Stir mixture well and let it stand for 10 minutes. Pour it into the pie crust.

Carefully roll out a pastry lid and place it on top of the pie. Slice 2–3 vent lines in the pastry lid (I do these along the same path I would cut it to serve). Brush the top of the shell with an egg wash (1 egg and a splash of milk mixed well).

Bake at 375 degrees for 30–40 minutes, until the crust is golden brown. Let the pie rest for several minutes before serving.

SOUR CREAM APPLE PIE

I first tried a sour cream apple pie at a family reunion, thinking it was just an average apple pie. It was amazing, and I asked what made it so different from most apple pies. I have to admit I was surprised to learn that sour cream is what made all the difference.

1 pie crust (pages 3–10)

3 cups thinly sliced, peeled, and deseeded apples

1 cup sour cream

1 egg

1½ cups white sugar

1 tsp. vanilla

½ tsp. salt

3 Tbsp. flour

1 tsp. cinnamon

After slicing the apples, mix the remaining ingredients well in a bowl. Add the apples and stir them in gently. Place the pie crust in a Dutch oven or a cast-iron skillet. Leave the edges long. Pour the apple mix into the pie shell and flatten the mixture out as best as you can.

If you are making a full-shell pie, Carefully lay the pie lid on top of the pie. Slice 2–3 vent lines in the pastry lid (I do these along the same path I would cut it to serve).

If you choose a lattice top, cut the lattice into strips and lay them out in one of the patterns found on page 19.

Brush the top of the shell with an egg wash (1 egg and a splash of milk mixed well).

Bake at 375 degrees for 30–40 minutes until the crust is golden brown. Let the pie rest for several minutes before serving.

APPLE CRUMB PIE

An apple crumb pie is similar to the Dutch Apple Pie (page 73), except for the crumble on top, which has a lot more crunch.

1 pie crust (see pages 3–10)

For the apples:
4 cups thinly sliced, peeled, and deseeded tart apples,
    such as Granny Smiths
1 cup brown sugar
½ cup sugar
1 tsp. cinnamon
3 Tbsp. flour
1 tsp. salt

For the topping:
⅓ cup flour
¼ cup oatmeal
½ cup brown sugar
1 tsp. cinnamon
8 Tbsp. real butter

Lay the prepared pie crust in a Dutch oven or a cast-iron skillet. Crimp the edges and set aside. In a separate bowl, mix the flour, oatmeal, brown sugar, and cinnamon for the topping and then cut the butter in with a pastry cutter. Set aside. Mix together the ingredients for the apples and lay them in the bottom of the pie shell. Bake at 375 degrees for 30 minutes. After 30 minutes, layer the crumble topping on top of the apples. Bake at 375 degrees for another 10–15 minutes. The crust should be a deep golden brown. Let the pie rest for several minutes before serving.

• PUMPKIN PIES •

Pumpkin pie is a symbol of fall, Thanksgiving, and family parties, because pumpkins are at their prime in the late fall. Today we can buy pumpkin puree in a can any time of the year, so I like to whip up a pumpkin pie whenever I can. I have included butternut squash and sweet potato pie recipes in this section. You'll find that they are similar to pumpkin pie, but with their own unique flavors and textures.

AMISH PUMPKIN PIE

This recipe goes way back. It is a silky custard version of pumpkin pie and is definitely a favorite of mine. In the fall, nothing is better than eating pumpkin pie with fresh whipped cream while watching a college football game.

   1 pie crust (see pages 3–10)

   1½ cups pureed pumpkin

   4 eggs

   ¾ cup brown sugar

   ¾ cup white sugar

   1 Tbsp. flour

   1 tsp. cinnamon

   ¼ tsp. nutmeg

   1 tsp. vanilla

   ¼ tsp. ginger

   1 cup cream

   ½ tsp. salt

Lay the prepared pie crust in a Dutch oven or a cast-iron skillet. In a bowl, mix all the ingredients. Pour into the open pie shell. Bake for 40 minutes. The custard should be set and not jiggle.

TWO-LAYER PUMPKIN PIE

This two-layer pumpkin pie is similar to the Creamy Pumpkin Pie (page 80). This pie is cool, creamy, and delicious.

For the crust:
2 (8-oz.) pkgs. graham crackers
¼ cup sugar
½ cup real butter

For the cream layer:
1 (8-oz.) pkg. cream cheese
1 cup thawed whipped topping
2 Tbsp. sugar
½ tsp. vanilla
1 Tbsp. milk

For the pumpkin:
¾ cup canned pumpkin puree
¼ cup cream
1 pkg. vanilla instant pudding mix
1½ cup thawed whipped topping
¼ tsp. nutmeg
1 tsp. allspice
1 tsp. cinnamon
¼ tsp. ginger
1 tsp. vanilla

Crush the graham crackers: If you have a food processor, this is a quick job (If you are gluten-intolerant, you can use corn flake crumbs). If you don't have a processor, keep the crackers in the package and pound them against the countertop. Mix the sugar and the graham crackers together. Melt the butter and mix into the graham crackers. Press the mixture into a the bottom and sides of a pie tin. Mix the ingredients together well for the cream layer and spoon it into the bottom of the pie shell. Place it in the fridge and let it set for 1 hour. Mix all the pumpkin ingredients together, pour them into the pie shell on top of the cream layer, and refrigerate for 2–3 hours until the pie is set.

BUTTERNUT SQUASH PIE

Far and away, this is my favorite of all the pumpkin-esque pies. I think the flavor of butternut squash is better than that of pumpkin. I like to make this pie with leftover squash. The toffee bits were an accident but turned out to be a great addition.

> 1 pie crust (see pages 3–10)
>
> 1½ cups baked and pureed butternut squash
>
> 4 eggs
>
> ¾ cup brown sugar
>
> ¾ cup white sugar
>
> 1 Tbsp. flour
>
> 1 tsp. cinnamon
>
> 1 tsp. allspice
>
> 1 tsp. vanilla
>
> ¼ tsp. ginger
>
> 1 cup cream
>
> ½ tsp. salt

Lay the prepared pie crust in a Dutch oven or a cast-iron skillet. In a bowl, mix all the ingredients. Pour into the open pie shell. Bake at 375 degrees for 40 minutes. The custard should be set and not jiggle.

CREAMY PUMPKIN PIE

This cold pumpkin pie is great. The recipe calls for a handmade graham cracker crust, but you can use a premade crust if you want to make the pie more quickly.

For the crust:
2 (8-oz.) pkgs. graham crackers
¼ cup white sugar
½ cup real butter

For the pumpkin:
1 cup canned pumpkin puree
½ cup cream
1 (2-oz.) pkg. vanilla instant pudding mix
2 cups thawed whipped topping
¼ tsp. nutmeg
1 tsp. allspice
1 tsp. cinnamon
¼ tsp. ginger
1 tsp. vanilla

Crush the graham crackers: If you have a food processor, this is a quick job (If you are gluten-intolerant, you can use corn flake crumbs). If you don't have a processor, keep the crackers in the package and pound them against the countertop. Mix the sugar and the graham crackers together. Melt the butter and add to the mixture. Press it into the sides and bottom of a pie tin.

Mix all the pumpkin ingredients together, pour them into the pie shell, and refrigerate for 2–3 hours until the pie has set.

SWEET POTATO PIE

Sweet potatoes are great for pie-making. The texture is a little bit different than a pumpkin pie, and it is a little sweeter.

1 pie crust (pages 3–10)

1¼ cups mashed sweet potatoes

4 eggs

½ cup brown sugar

½ cup white sugar

1 Tbsp. flour

1 tsp. cinnamon

1 tsp. allspice

1 tsp. vanilla

¼ tsp. ginger

1 cup milk

½ tsp. salt

Lay the prepared pie crust in a Dutch oven or cast-iron skillet. In a bowl, mix all the ingredients. Pour into the open pie shell.

Bake at 375 degrees for 40 minutes. The custard should be set and not jiggle.

• CUSTARD PIES •

Custards are simply a mix of eggs, dairy, and sugar. Any flavors can be added to a custard.

CUSTARD PUMPKIN PIE

This is similar to a traditional pumpkin pie in flavor. Though all pumpkin pies are a type of custard, this pie is lighter in texture than a classic pumpkin pie.

1 pie crust (see pages 3–10)
¾ cup pureed pumpkin
4 eggs
¾ cup white sugar
3 Tbsp. flour
1 tsp. cinnamon
¼ tsp. nutmeg
1 tsp. vanilla
¼ tsp. ginger
1 cup cream
½ tsp. salt

Lay the prepared pie shell in a Dutch oven or cast-iron skillet. In a bowl mix all the ingredients. Pour into the open pie shell.

Bake for 40 minutes. The custard should be set and not jiggle.

CRÈME BRÛLÉE PIE

Crème Brûlée has remained one of my all-time favorite desserts. It is a very silky, incredibly rich custard Tempering the eggs is important for the texture—follow the directions exactly and you won't have any problems.

1 pie crust (pages 3–10)

1 pint cream

1 tsp. cinnamon

6 egg yolks

1 cup sugar, divided

1 tsp. vanilla

Place the prepared pie crust in a Dutch oven or a cast-iron skillet. Crimp the edges and use a fork to poke holes in the pie shell. Bake the empty shell for 15–20 minutes, until it is starting to brown lightly. Heat the cream and cinnamon in a saucepan on medium heat until it is just starting to bubble and steam (205 degrees).

In the meantime, mix the egg yolks, ½ cup sugar, and vanilla together. When the cream starts to bubble slightly, remove it from the heat. To temper the eggs, ladle a small scoop of the hot cream into the egg yolks while stirring it vigorously with a whisk. Continue spooning the cream into the eggs while whisking until all the cream is in the egg yolks. Pour mixture immediately into the pie shell and bake at 300 degrees for 20 minutes.

Afterward, check the pie by shaking it. It should be like a well-set gelatin. If it is still loose, continue to cook it until it sets. Let the pie relax for at least 1 hour—it is best if chilled in the fridge. Sprinkle the remaining sugar on top of the pie and use a small propane torch or candy butane torch to melt the sugar until it is brown and bubbly.

BUTTERMILK PIE

I first tried a buttermilk pie was at a barbecue joint called Mark's Feed Store in Louisville, Kentucky. I had never heard of a buttermilk pie and thought I was taking a real chance by ordering it. Turns out it was the star of the show. My friend and I ordered a second helping to go. The pie was drizzled with a coulis of freshly picked strawberries. It has taken me a while to figure out how to make this pie and do it justice, but at long last I succeeded.

1 pie crust (see pages 3–10)

For the custard:
4 eggs
8 Tbsp. real butter, softened
¾ cup buttermilk
½ cup cream
4 Tbsp. flour
2 cups sugar
1 tsp. vanilla
1 Tbsp. sherry vinegar

For the strawberry coulis:
2 cups strawberries sliced thin lengthwise
½ cup white sugar
1 Tbsp. cornstarch
1 tsp. sherry vinegar

Lay the prepared pie shell in a Dutch oven or cast-iron skillet. Crimp the edges and set aside. Mix all the ingredients for the custard and pour into the pie shell. Bake at 375 degrees for 55 minutes, until the custard is set and jiggles like a well-set gelatin. Remove the pie and let it set for at least 20 minutes. In the meantime, place all the ingredients for the coulis in a saucepan on medium heat (A true coulis will be run through a food processor—feel free to do so). Stir until the sugar is dissolved and the liquid boils and thickens. Let the coulis cool down for 5 minutes. Drizzle the coulis over the slices of buttermilk pie to serve.

KEY LIME PIE

I love key lime pie. You can find key limes in most Latin markets, and at the occasional grocery store The taste of key limes is truly unique and wonderful. If you can find them, they will give your pie a special flavor that you can't get from regular limes.

1 pie crust (see pages 3–10)

6 egg yolks

1 (14-oz.) can sweetened condensed milk

½ cup key lime juice

1 tsp. key lime zest

Place the prepared pie crust in a Dutch oven or a cast-iron skillet. Crimp the edges and use a fork to poke holes in the pie shell. Cover the pie shell with foil and fill the pie with dried beans or rice; otherwise, the pastry will collect at the bottom of the pan, leaving you with nothing on the sides.

Bake the empty shell for 15–20 minutes, until it is starting to brown lightly. Mix all the ingredients together. Pour into the pie shell and bake at 325 degrees for 20 minutes. Check the pie by shaking it. It should be set like gelatin. If it is not set, continue cooking and checking until it is. Let the pie rest for at least 1 hour before serving.

• PUDDING PIES •

BANANA CREAM PIE

I love a banana cream pie. When I was in the South, I had quite a few of them made with vanilla wafers on the top. Tempering the eggs in this recipe is important for the pudding texture.

1 pie crust (see pages 3–10)

2 Tbsp. real butter

1½ cups whole milk

1 cup cream

2 cups sugar

1 tsp. vanilla

½ tsp. salt

3½ Tbsp. cornstarch

6 egg yolks

2 bananas

fresh whipped cream

Place the prepared pie crust in a Dutch oven or a cast-iron skillet. Crimp the edges and use a fork to poke holes in the pie shell. Cover the pie shell with foil and fill the pie with dried beans or rice; otherwise, the pastry will collect at the bottom of the pan, leaving you with nothing on the sides.

Bake the empty shell for 15–20 minutes, until it is starting to brown lightly. In a saucepan, mix the butter, milk, cream, sugar, vanilla, salt, and cornstarch. Bring to a boil on medium-high heat until the mixture thickens.

In the meantime, mix the egg yolks thoroughly in a bowl. When the liquid in the saucepan is hot and thick, ladle it into the egg yolks one spoonful at a time, whisking it vigorously.

Pour mixture into the pie shell and bake at 325 degrees for 35 minutes. Check the pie by shaking it. It should be set like a well-set gelatin. If it is not set, continue cooking and checking until it is. Let the pie relax for at least 1 hour and then place it in the fridge for several hours or overnight.

Peel and slice the bananas and place them on top of the pie. Serve with fresh whipped cream.

GERMAN CHOCOLATE PIE

This recipe was adapted from the famous and well-loved german chocolate cake. I think it's just as good, if not better.

1 pie crust (see pages 3–10)

For the chocolate layer:
2 Tbsp. real butter
½ cup milk
1 cup cream
½ cup sugar
1½ tsp. vanilla
3 Tbsp. cornstarch
4 oz. nice dark chocolate (do not use inexpensive stuff; it doesn't work well)
3 egg yolks

For the coconut caramel layer:
1 (5-oz.) can evaporated milk
1 egg, beaten
½ cup sugar
½ tsp. salt
5 Tbsp. real butter
1 cup shredded coconut
½ cup finely chopped pecans

Place the prepared pie crust in a Dutch oven or a cast-iron skillet. Crimp the edges and use a fork to poke holes in the pie shell. Cover the pie shell with foil and fill with dried beans or rice; otherwise the pastry will collect at the bottom of the pan, leaving you with nothing on the sides.

Bake the empty shell for 20–30 minutes, until it is golden brown.

Make the chocolate layer: in a saucepan, mix the butter, milk, cream, sugar, vanilla, and cornstarch. Bring to a boil on medium-high heat until the mixture thickens. Turn off the heat. Stir in the chocolate.

In the meantime, mix the egg yolks in a bowl until they are well mixed. When the liquid in the saucepan is hot and thick, ladle it into the egg yolks one spoonful at a time, whisking it vigorously as you do so. Pour into the pie shell and let it cool.

Make the coconut caramel layer: In another saucepan, cook the evaporated milk, egg, sugar, salt, and butter. Cook on medium heat until the mixture is thick and bubbly. Slowly stir in the coconut and pecans. Let the caramel cool down for several minutes.

Pour the caramel on top of the chocolate layer in the pie. Let the pie cool down for 1 hour before serving.

LEMON MERINGUE PIE

This classic pie works great in a Dutch oven. There is no substitute for fresh lemons. You can also make a key lime pie with this same recipe: use 8–10 key limes instead of lemons.

1 pie crust (see pages 3–10)
3 Tbsp. flour
3 Tbsp. cornstarch
1½ cups sugar
½ tsp. salt
1½ cups water
zest and juice of 3 lemons
2 Tbsp. butter
3 eggs, separated

For the meringue:
3 egg whites
½ tsp. vanilla
¼ tsp. cream of tartar
6 Tbsp. sugar

Begin by blind-baking an egg-glazed, open pie shell for 15 minutes in the Dutch oven. The crust should be golden. In the bottom of a Dutch oven, mix together the flour, cornstarch, sugar, salt, and water. Whisk together well and cook it until mixture is thick and bubbly. Remove it from the heat. In a bowl, mix together the egg yolks. Gradually stir in a little of the filling to temper the eggs. Pour the eggs into the filling. Bring to a soft boil. Remove from the heat. Stir in slowly the lemon zest, lemon juice, and butter. Pour filling into the pie shell in the Dutch oven. For the meringue, mix the egg whites, vanilla, and cream of tartar. Whip mixture until soft peaks form. Gradually add the sugar 1 tablespoon at a time, whipping it. The mixture should form stiff, glossy peaks, and the sugar should be dissolved. Spread over top of the warm pie filling. Bake for 15 minutes at 375 degrees. The meringue should be starting to brown.

• NUT PIES •

SOUTHERN BUTTER CARAMEL PECAN PIE

While traveling through the South, I fell in love with pecan pie. A lot of this love came from the fresh pecans growing all over the region. I have tried a number of recipes and this is the one I like best. It is not the most healthy recipe, but it's great for a once-in-a-while treat.

1 pie crust (see pages 3–10)

4 eggs, slightly beaten

1 cup dark corn syrup

2/3 cup sugar

½ cup butter, melted

1 tsp. vanilla

1¼ cups chopped pecans or pecan halves

Place the prepared pie crust in a Dutch oven or a cast-iron skillet. Mix the ingredients together and pour into the open-faced pie shell. Bake for 35–40 minutes. Like a custard pie, when it's done it will be firm when jiggled.

PRALINES AND CREAM PIE

This is the only chilled nut pie on my menu and it is amazing. Once you try it, you are going to love it.

For the crust:

2 (8-oz.) pkgs. graham crackers

¼ cup sugar

½ cup real butter

For the filling:

4 oz. cream cheese, room temperature

¼ cup cream

1 (2-oz.) pkg. vanilla instant pudding mix

2 cups thawed whipped topping

1 tsp. vanilla

4 oz. chopped praline pecans

¼ cup caramel sundae topping

Crush the graham crackers: If you have a food processor, this is a quick job (if you are gluten intolerant, you can use corn flake crumbs). If you don't have a processor, keep the crackers in the package and pound them against the countertop.

Mix the sugar and graham crackers together. Melt the butter and mix into the graham crackers. Press the mixture into the bottom and sides of a pie tin. Mix the cream cheese, cream, pudding mix, whipped topping, and vanilla well. Fold the pralines and caramel into the cream and pudding mix.

Carefully pour the mixture into the pie shell and refrigerate for 2–3 hours until the pie is set.

CHOCOLATE CARAMEL MACADAMIA PIE

Once my daughter was competing in a Dutch oven competition and she needed to come up with a dessert to bake. She thought that a caramel macadamia pie sounded good. We tried it out and fell in love with it. I have always been such a fan of the Mauna Loa candies that everyone brings back from Hawaii, and this pie tastes just like them.

1 pie crust (see pages 3–10)

4 eggs, slightly beaten

1 cup dark corn syrup

$^2/_3$ cup sugar

½ cup butter, melted

1 tsp. vanilla

1¼ cups chopped macadamia nuts

¾ cup semisweet chocolate chips

Place the prepared pie crust in a Dutch oven or cast-iron skillet. Mix all the ingredients together except the chocolate chips and pour mixture into the open-faced pie shell.

Bake for 35–40 minutes. Like a custard pie, it should be firm when jiggled. Remove the pie from the oven and immediately sprinkle the chocolate chips on the top. Let the pie relax for 20 minutes before serving.

SALTED CARAMEL CASHEW PIE

As much as I love a caramel pecan pie, I like caramel cashew better. The directions are similar, but the final product is quite different.

1 pie crust (see pages 3–10)

3 eggs, slightly beaten

1 cup light corn syrup

½ cup sugar

½ cup + 2 Tbsp. real butter, melted

1 tsp. vanilla

1¼ cups cashew chunks and pieces

1½ tsp. sea salt

Place the prepared pie crust in a Dutch oven or cast-iron skillet. Mix the ingredients together and pour it into the open-faced pie shell.

Bake for 35–40 minutes. Like a custard pie, it should be firm when jiggled.

6

NONTRADITIONAL PIES

I decided to include a couple nontraditional pies in this book, just for fun. I know that a shepherd's pie is not a real pie, but it has pie in the name, so I had to include it. I've included some other recipes that use pastry crusts, like empanadas. And tarts are really just miniature pies with a fresh fruit topping.

SHEPHERD'S PIE

Shepherd's pie originated in the United Kingdom. The traditional pie was made with ground mutton, hence the name. A mixture of ground beef and pork are substituted for mutton in this recipe because they are far easier to find. If you have access to ground mutton, feel free to use it instead.

For the potato layer:

2 lbs. russet potatoes

½ cup cream

2 tsp. salt

1 tsp. pepper

4 Tbsp. real butter

8 oz. Cheddar cheese, shredded

For the meat layer:

1 lb. ground beef

½ lb. ground pork

1 small onion, cut into slivers

2 Tbsp. real butter

2 cloves garlic, minced

1 cup cut and washed fresh green beans

1 (14-oz.) can crushed tomatoes

¼ cup shredded Parmesan cheese

1½ tsp. salt

Boil the potatoes until tender. Strain the liquid and add all of the ingredients for the potato layer except the cheese. Mash well with a masher. Set aside. In a Dutch oven or skillet, sauté the onions in 2 tablespoons of butter until they are starting to brown. Add the beef, garlic, salt, and pork to the onions and brown the meat well. Stir in the tomatoes and green beans and simmer on medium heat for 5 minutes. Remove from the heat. Stir in the Parmesan cheese. In a Dutch oven or deep cast-iron skillet, spread the meat layer on the bottom. Place the potatoes on top and cover with Cheddar cheese. Bake at 400 degrees for 15–20 minutes. The top of the potatoes should be browning and the cheese bubbly and beginning to brown.

CREAM CHEESE FRUIT PIE

My family ate a lot of these cream cheese and fruit pies growing up. We usually used a crust made from corn flake crumbs, but I like it better with a pastry crust. You can use any fresh fruit in this recipe.

1 pie crust (see pages 3–10)

For the fruit:
2 cups strawberries sliced thin lengthwise
1 cup sugar
2 Tbsp. cornstarch
1 tsp. sherry vinegar

For the filling:
8 oz. cream cheese, room temperature
½ cup powdered sugar
½ pint whipping cream
1 tsp. vanilla

Place the prepared pie crust in a Dutch oven or a cast-iron skillet. Crimp the edges and use a fork to poke holes in the pie shell. Cover the pie shell with foil and fill with dried beans or rice; otherwise, the pastry will collect at the bottom of the pan, leaving you with nothing on the sides. Bake the empty shell for 20–30 minutes, until it is golden brown. Let the pie crust cool.

Mix together the ingredients for the filling. Whip them for several minutes on high speed. Fill the pie shell with the cream mixture. Set it in the fridge for at least an hour to allow the filling to set. In the meantime, place all the ingredients for the fruit in a saucepan. Heat it on medium-high, stirring occasionally until the mixture is boiling and thickens. Let the fruit cool—it is best chilled. Spread the fruit mixture across the top of each slice directly before serving.

EMPANADAS

Empanadas are simply turnovers made from pastry. They can be filled with sweet or savory fillings—I have seen them filled with everything from beef to pumpkin. This recipe is from Argentina.

1 pie crust (see pages 3–10)

1 lb. beefsteak (like skirt meat or flank steak), cut into thin strips

juice of 1 pink grapefruit (½ cup)

1 small onion, cut into strips

2 tsp. salt

1 tsp. black pepper

2–3 small red potatoes, cubed, skins on

½ cup chopped green olives

½ cup chopped hard-boiled eggs

1 cup sour cream

The night before, mix the steak, grapefruit juice, onion, salt, and pepper together. Place them in a plastic bag and set them in the fridge to marinate. The next day, prepare the pastry crust. Sauté the steak and marinade in a skillet. When the liquid is almost gone, add the potatoes and continue cooking until the meat is well browned. Let the mixture cool down. Add the green olives, hard boiled eggs, and sour cream. Fold the mixture together.

Roll out the pastry and cut into circles anywhere from 2 to 4 inches in diameter (whatever your size preference is). Place some of the filling in the center of each circle and fold it in half. Crimp the edges.

Bake them together, seam side up, in the Dutch oven at 375 degrees for 20–30 minutes, until the crust is golden brown.

FRUIT TARTS

Fruit tarts are so called because fresh fruit can make these pastries a little bit tart. The key to making tarts is to fill a shallow ramekin with pastry cream. For this recipe I use fresh fruit. If you would like to top it with a sweet coulis, follow the recipe for Buttermilk Pie (page 82).

1 pie crust (see pages 3–10)

For the pastry cream:
1½ cups milk
6 egg yolks, room temperature
1 cup sugar
3 Tbsp. cornstarch
1 tsp. vanilla
2 Tbsp. cream
fresh fruit of choice, sliced thin (or a fruit coulis)

Heat the milk in a saucepan until it is starting to bubble around the edges. In the meantime, mix the egg yolks and the sugar until mixture is thickened. Add the cornstarch. Slowly ladle the scalded milk into the egg yolks a little at a time to temper the eggs. Pour the entire mixture into a saucepan and cook over medium heat, stirring constantly until the mixture thickens like a pudding. When the mixture is thick and bubbly, whisk it well and stir in the vanilla and cream.

Cover the pastry cream with plastic wrap and place it in the fridge until chilled. It can be kept in the fridge for several days and used as needed. Prepare a pastry crust and roll it out thin. Fill shallow ramekins with the pastry, making sure it fills into the contours of the dish. Bake at 350 degrees for 15 minutes, until lightly browned. When the pie shells have cooled down, dump them carefully out of the ramekins. Fill with pastry cream and top with fresh sliced fruit or a fruit coulis.

INDEX

ABOUT THE AUTHOR

Matt Pelton grew up in central Utah where he learned the art of Dutch oven cooking. He brought his passion with him on a two-year mission to Boston for The Church of Jesus Christ of Latter-day Saints; he packed his ten-inch Dutch oven in his suitcase. At every opportunity, he learned to cook food from the many cultures in the Boston area. When he returned home, he met and married his wife of fourteen years, Katie. They have three wonderful children: Megan, Tristan, and Braxton. Matt was bitten by the bug of competitive cooking and has competed in the Kansas City Barbecue Society pro-division barbecue competitions. He also competes in the International Dutch Oven Society's advanced cooking circuit where he and his cooking partner, Doug Martin, won the 2012 IDOS World Championship. Matt travels around the West competing and teaching Dutch oven classes. His previous books are *From Mountaintop to Tabletop*, *The Cast Iron Chef*, *The Cast Iron Gourmet*, and *Up in Smoke*.